YOU DON'T
HAVE TO BE OLD
WHEN YOU
GROW OLD

YOU DON'T HAVE TO BE OLD WHEN YOU GROW OLD

by Florence M. Taylor

Logos International
Plainfield, New Jersey

Excerpts from the following publications were reprinted by permission of the publishers:

God of a Hundred Names, Barbara Greene and Victor Golancz. (Garden City, New York: Doubleday, 1963).

The Christian's Secret of a Happy Life, Hannah Whitall Smith. (Westwood, New Jersey: Fleming H. Revell, 1952).

"Life in These United States," *Reader's Digest* (March, 1967).

Thou Art My God, Florence M. Taylor. (Norwalk, Connecticut: The C.R. Gibson Company).

Harper's Bible Dictionary, Madeline S. and J. Lane Miller. ©1952, 1954, 1955, 1956, 1958, 1959, 1961, 1973 by Harper & Row, Publishers, Inc.

From Everlasting to Everlasting: Promises and Prayers Selected from the Bible, Florence M. Taylor. (New York: The Seabury Press, 1973).

Treasury of the Christian Faith, Stanley I. Stuber and Thomas C. Clark, eds. (New York: Association Press, 1949).

In the Morning, Bread: Devotions for the New Day, selected by Florence M. Taylor. (New Canaan, Connecticut: Keats Publishing, Inc., special contents copyright, 1976, by Florence M. Taylor).

J.B. Phillips: The New Testament in Modern English, Revised Edition. ©J.B. Phillips, 1958, 1960, 1972. (New York: The Macmillan Company).

The Revised Standard Version of the Bible, copyrighted 1946, 1952, ©1971, 1973.

All Scripture references,
unless otherwise noted,
are taken from the King James Version.

Contents

PART IV A FAITH FOR OLD AGE

This book is dedicated to
my family—

to my grandparents
all of whom I remember with deep affection:
Henry and Catherine Tompkins
Alexander and Elizabeth Flandreau

to my husband's parents:
John and "Libbie" Taylor

to my parents:
Edward and "Tette" Tompkins

to my three children and their mates:
Ed and Kay, Bette and Will, Peg and Bob

to my nine grandchildren:
Bill, Bob, Tom, Tora, Margaret, David,
Greg, Ted, Arthur

to my three great-grandchildren:
Christine, William and Jennifer

and to other great-grandchildren
still to come:

with inexpressible gratitude to God
for their share in my life,
and for His faithfulness to all generations.

Know therefore that the Lord thy God,
he is God, the faithful God,
which keepeth covenant and mercy with them
that love him and keep his commandments
to a thousand generations. (Deuteronomy 7:9)

Preface

It was just about ten years ago that I wrote the little book, *The Autumn Years*, in an attempt to share with others in my generation some of the insights that I had acquired in three-quarters of a century of busy living.

Today as I read over that book, I am amazed to realize how much deeper and more satisfying is my spiritual life now than it was even a brief ten years ago. And so I have been moved to rewrite the earlier book, this time in terms of the *winter* years, in order to share with my contemporaries some of these later insights and meditations.

In a sense this is my personal testimony to God's goodness and reality; and I pray that He will use this book to draw closer to himself many weary, discouraged and lonely souls in the later years of their lives, and to flood their hearts with an awareness of His presence, and the joy that He alone can give.

Thou wilt shew me the path of life: in thy presence is fulness of joy; at thy right hand there are pleasures for evermore. (Psalm 16:11)

YOU DON'T HAVE TO BE OLD WHEN YOU GROW OLD

PART I

Old Age: Its Difficulties

1

Shock

Old age, it seems to me, always comes as a complete surprise. In spite of all one's years of living, in spite of one's unavoidable recognition of the passing years, old age itself is always a shock.

I remember when I was a little girl, I overheard my mother say to her sister, soon after the death of my last grandparents, "Liz, doesn't it seem strange? We're the old people now!"

I also remember when the realization of my own old age broke upon my consciousness. I was in a department store, and I saw in a mirror the image of an old gray-haired woman passing between the counters. With a sudden icy shock of realization, I exclaimed to myself, unbelievingly and ungrammatically, "Why, that's *me!*"

My husband used to tell with grim amusement a similar moment of revelation. He was a sturdy, vigorous seventy at the time, and because of a heart condition had given up driving, on his doctor's recommendation. He was far from immobilized, however, and thought nothing of hiking several miles. Often our three-year-old grandson accompanied him, usually riding in his go-cart. One day they went to a hardware store on an errand, and my husband inadvertently left a small package on the counter. He went back for it later. The package was still on the counter, with a note on it: "This belongs to the old man with the baby carriage"!

Another relevant incident that I recall with amusement, albeit with a degree of tender appreciation, occurred at a summer conference. I was over seventy at the time, and was enjoying myself tremendously. A young seminary student, not long out of his teens, showed a preference for my company that was, to say the least, flattering. He would join a group and deliberately choose to sit next to me, and we had a number of brief but interesting conversations.

One day near the end of the conference, I was sitting alone under a tree, reading, when he came over and sat beside me. For a while he did not say anything, and neither did I; we just sat in a companionable silence. Then he broke out impulsively, "You know, it's been great, hasn't it? I mean, I guess you're the oldest person here, aren't you? And I'm the youngest. And, well, what I mean is, it's been nice knowing you!"

"Thank you," I said, humbly realizing that I had been given, across age barriers which often prove insurmountable, a rare gift of friendship.

Shock

Probably no one accepts the fact of his own old age until he sees some recognition of it reflected in those around him. But sooner or later the truth cannot be evaded or denied.

We may comfort ourselves a bit with the assurance that, as a leader of a conference once exclaimed: "What do you mean, the aging? *Everybody's* aging, even a newborn baby!" But, undeniably, some of us are considerably farther along in the aging process than others.

To all of us in due time and, always I feel sure, with a sense of shock, comes the realization: "Why! We're the old people now!"

2

Circles–Expanding and Contracting

Each of us inevitably seems to himself much of the time to be the center of the universe. From the moment our awakening consciousness becomes aware of our surroundings, our life develops in widening circles, from the close confinement of the mother's womb, to the only slightly less protective encirclement of her arms, on out into the home surroundings, and into widening circles of consciousness in the community, the country, the world, and finally in awareness of the illimitable universe of which we are a part.

Developing human beings respond in various ways to these new areas of experience and activity. Some meet each new experience with a feeling of uneasiness and discomfort; each expanding area presents a threat, each change becomes something to dread. Others are able to welcome the new and the strange with a sense of anticipation and delight in adventure.

The attitude of joyous expectancy has a great deal to do with successful adjustment to new situations, new responsibilities. The child going to school, the young person going away to college, the man or woman entering the world of business or profession, the bride and groom starting their life together—all these are helped by an attitude of confidence and joy.

Now in all the history of civilization, no approach to the mystery of life has ever been so characterized by confident hope and expectancy as has that of the Christian faith. Here is no philosophy based on wishful thinking. Here is an acceptance of life as it is, with clear-eyed recognition of the reality of evil, and sin, and suffering. But here also is an unshakable belief that God is in control; that He uses even the most tragic happenings of our lives to forward His eternal purposes; that in His gift of His Son Jesus He has provided for the forgiveness of our sins, and for our gradual transformation, "from glory unto glory," into the likeness of His Son; that through His Holy Spirit indwelling us, He has made it possible for us to face triumphantly the worst that life can do to us; and that in our assurance of eternal life through the resurrection of Jesus, He has taken away even the fear of death itself, either for ourselves or for our loved ones. No wonder the believing Christian is radiant with love and hope and faith! Praise God!

Surely at no other period in our lives is our Christian faith so important to us, as in these closing years, these "winter" years.

It is easy, but profoundly unwise, to accept our modern

society's evaluation of old age as a time of idleness, senility, and uselessness, as years of inactivity and boredom.

True it is, that at some point in our development there comes the realization that the expanding circles of our physical existence have reversed their direction, have begun to contract, closer and closer, until for many at last they have narrowed to the dimensions of a single room. This much we must accept. But it is also true that some rare souls seem able to cope with the reality of the contracting physical circles without suffering any diminution of their spiritual interests and concerns. They are the dauntless ones who witness to the truth that

> Stone walls do not a prison make,
> Nor iron bars a cage.
> Richard Lovelace (1618-1658)

Theoretically at least, the widening *spiritual* circles continue indefinitely. How beautifully Oliver Wendell Holmes has expressed this idea in his "The Chambered Nautilus"!

> Year after year beheld the silent toil
>   That spread his lustrous coil;
>   Still, as the spiral grew,
> He left the past year's dwelling for the new,
> Stole with soft step its shining archway through,
>   Built up its idle door,
> Stretched in his last-found home, and knew the
>   old no more.

Build thee more stately mansions, O my soul,
  As the swift seasons roll!
  Leave thy low-vaulted past.
Let each new temple, nobler than the last,
Shut thee from heaven with a dome more vast,
  Till thou at length art free,
Leaving thine outgrown shell by life's unresting
sea.

Surely the building of "more stately mansions" must not cease with the years of lessened physical activity. What finer concern could engage our hearts and minds during these later years than the gradual escape from our "low-vaulted past" into that greater freedom which sees even death as a joyous adventure of faith?

The rightness and wholesomeness of this attitude seems obvious. Our hearts and minds expand to greater depths of understanding, greater and more spiritual insights, until, in God's good time, we emerge from this physical existence into some unimaginable realization of freedom and truth and eternal joyous activity in dimensions far exceeding our finite human understandings.

3

The "Poor Me's"

I had an old auntie who used to shake her head sadly over my querulous complaints, and murmur, "My, oh my! You surely do have a bad case of the 'poor me's.'"

"Poor me! I haven't anything to do!" "Poor me! Nobody likes me." "Poor me! Do I *have* to go to bed *now*?" "Poor me! Do I *have* to dry the dishes?"

Children are not the only ones who develop bad cases of the "poor me's." It's a disease especially liable to attack old people.

"Poor me! I never slept a wink all night!" "Poor me! Everybody mumbles nowadays!" "Poor me! Nobody wants me around!" "Poor me! My arthritis is almost unbearable!" And so on and on and on.

"Good morning, Grandma. How are you today?" is *not* an invitation to a long description of aches and pains. What is indicated is a cheerful, "Fine, thanks!" Or if you have a sensitive conscience that objects to this as an untruth, perhaps you can recognize that this is a rhetorical question that needs no direct answer, and contrive a truthful response that changes the subject. "Good morning! What a lovely day!" Or "Good morning! That was quite a storm last night."

All of which in no sense denies the seeming justification for the "poor me's." It *is* miserable to toss and turn, sleepless, hour after hour. It *is* hard to stand the constant gnawing pain of arthritis. To be in the midst of a group and unable to hear what people say, or to half hear and miss the punch line of the joke or the crux of the conversation, is an exasperating experience. I do not know a single old person who could not describe a list of complaints that would be reason enough to make a saint gloomy.

Only the saints never are gloomy. They are the rare souls who live joyously and triumphantly in the midst of all their sufferings. They are the blessed ones who spread the contagion of mental health and happiness. Theirs is a skill of living well—worth acquiring at any age, especially in old age—the ability to master and control gloomy emotions.

Psychologists tell us that emotion produces action, but also that action produces emotion. We are afraid, and so we run away. But equally true is the fact that we are afraid *because* we run away.

Act as though you are happy, and you'll be happy. Smile, and some of the gloom will be dissipated. Count your blessings, and suddenly you will find true gratitude welling up in your heart. Act as though you are unafraid, and genuine courage will take you by surprise.

This mastery of our coward moods would be far less important if it were a matter that concerned only our own happiness or unhappiness. But this is never true. Mood contagion is a tremendously powerful force.

A tired, discouraged mother creates in her children the very tensions and irritabilities which cause her tiredness. A gloomy grandparent, grumping and complaining, can spread the contagion of ill humor through the whole family and completely dissipate the normal, happy atmosphere of the family life.

Not many months ago, the Lord dealt with me decisively in this area of self-pity. It had to do with an interrupted nap.

I live in an expanded family consisting of my daughter, her doctor-husband, their four children (the youngest now sixteen) and several young people in need of a temporary Christian home for various reasons. My room is a delightful one, with windows on three sides. Beneath it is a porch; and over it on the third floor is another porch, an open one with a parapet around it.

On this particular day, I had come to my room after lunch for my usual nap. But today was Saturday, and as I settled down on my bed, I realized that some unusual noise was disturbing me. It developed that my two grandsons were down in the yard just below my windows, and that two of the other boys were up on the third floor porch over my head. They were joyously engaged in a game where the two in the yard were throwing a basketball up to the two on the porch, who were attempting to catch it in a metal scrapbasket! It is incredible what an amount of noise four healthy young people so occupied can produce!

I started to feel very sorry for myself! "With the whole yard to play in, *why* do they have to congregate right where I want to sleep?" I plumped up my pillow angrily, and stretched out again. And it was then that "the still, small voice" spoke compellingly in my innermost being: "So I suppose you'd rather be in an old people's home, where you could be all alone to nap whenever you wanted to, where there wouldn't be any young hoodlums to disturb you." But I had heard enough! "No!" I said out loud. "No! No! No! Lord, I repent! I'm sorry I complained! I *love* having them around. I know I'm the most blessed of octogenarians, to be living in the midst of my wonderful family! And I'm truly grateful."

And it was at that precise moment that there was a *crash*! The ball had come against the window directly beside my bed, fragmenting a small pane of glass, and showering me with the splinters. I got up, and as I shook the glass bits out of my clothing, I said out loud (shall I confess it?), "Well, *really*, Lord!" I expected to find myself bleeding copiously, but I couldn't find so much as a pinprick!

The crash had been followed by an appalled silence outside. Then suddenly all four of the young people catapulted into my room, eyes bulging, faces white and scared. There was a babble of voices: "Gay-Gay! You all right? Did it cut you? Gee, we're sorry!" I took one look at their frightened faces and burst out laughing.

After I had assured them that I was not hurt, they scurried around shaking the glass out of the bedclothes, bringing the vacuum cleaner, and generally getting in each other's way—and I decided I didn't want a nap anyway.

But there was an interesting aftermath to the incident. For the next two weeks or so, everyone who came to the house was regaled with the story of the broken window, and, each time, whichever of the boys was telling it ended up with the comment, "And you know what? Gay-Gay *just laughed!*" And I basked in their approval. But secretly I wondered what would have happened if the ball had hit the window five minutes sooner, before the Lord had dealt with me in so surprising a fashion.

"But I can't *always* be happy!" No, of course not. Who does not sometimes need the release from tension that a good cry brings? But at least, when those times come, we can cry by ourselves, in secret. We would never deliberately expose our family or those around us to the infection of a contagious disease, but we are often guilty of exposing them to the well nigh irresistible contagion of unhappiness, of ill humor, of gloominess and bitterness.

How blessed it is when we learn to share our joy, but hide our sorrow; to share our faith, but hide our doubts; to share our love, to pour it out liberally through every personal contact, freely, ungrudgingly, asking nothing in return! How we can rejoice that love, too, is irresistibly contagious! One truly loving person can sweeten and restore innumerable broken relationships.

Love is patient and kind. . . .
Love does not insist on its own way; it is not irritable or resentful. . . .
Love bears all things. . . .
Make love your aim. (1 Corinthians 13:4-5, 7; 14:1 RSV)

4

Bereavement

One of the causes of unhappiness in the latter years of life is bereavement. Whether it is the death of a mate, of a member of the family, or of a dearly loved friend, the feeling of emptiness created by the passing of a loved one is surely one of life's most difficult experiences. And no one ever lives to an advanced old age without having to face this experience over and over again.

Blessed are we in the midst of these sorrows, if we have already availed ourselves of our priceless treasure as Christians, in the holy companionship of the Father God, of His Son, Jesus Christ, and of the Holy Spirit indwelling us. Excessive grief, we discover, is always self-centered. We need to shift the focus of our thinking. This is a time we need to saturate our minds with the biblical promises:

The righteous cry, and the Lord heareth, and

delivereth them out of all their troubles. The Lord is nigh unto them that are of a broken heart. (Psalm 34:17-18)

Sing unto the Lord, O ye saints of his, and give thanks at the remembrance of his holiness. . . . Weeping may endure for a night, but joy cometh in the morning. (Psalm 30:4-5)

He healeth the broken in heart, and bindeth up their wounds. (Psalm 147:3)

For whether we live, we live unto the Lord; and whether we die, we die unto the Lord: whether we live therefore, or die, we are the Lord's. For to this end Christ both died, and rose, and revived, that he might be Lord both of the dead and living. (Romans 14:8-9)

For this corruptible must put on incorruption, and this mortal must put on immortality. So when this corruptible shall have put on incorruption, and this mortal shall have put on immortality, then shall be brought to pass the saying that is written, Death is swallowed up in victory. O death, where is thy sting? O grave, where is thy victory? . . . Thanks be to God, which giveth us the victory through our Lord Jesus Christ. (1 Corinthians 15:53-57)

And I heard a great voice out of heaven saying, Behold, the tabernacle of God is with men, and he will dwell with them, and they shall be his people, and God himself shall be with them, and be their God. And God shall wipe away all tears from their eyes; and there shall be no more death, neither sorrow, nor crying, neither shall there be any more pain: for the former things are passed away. . . . Behold, I make all things new. (Revelation 21:3-5)

5

We've Had Our Turn

Some of my pleasantest memories are connected with Grandma Taylor's cottage at the seashore. By the side of the house was a fine long swing, hung between two huge, upended logs.

All the children and young people of the community used the swing as if it were their own with almost complete freedom. Grandma was never far away; and whenever a dispute arose as to whose turn it was, suddenly she would appear, usually to chase away the older ones, so that the smaller ones might have their turn.

Three-year-old Ruthie, who lived a few houses away, soon learned who her champion was. Whenever she arrived at the swing, no matter how many children were there ahead of her, she would take one look, toddle over to the cottage door, pound with her chubby fist, and sing-song over and over until Grandma appeared: "Tayl', my tu'n! Tayl', my tu'n!"

"It's my turn now!" How old was I, I wonder, when I first heard or used that imperious demand? What a long and difficult task it is to learn the fairness and necessity of taking turns! Do we ever really learn it? Isn't it true that at the end of three-quarters of a century we are still resisting its inevitable imperative?

For years it was our turn to hold positions of leadership, and influence, and authority. But now it is the turn of others. Why does the important executive resent the younger assistant with new and different ideas?

That committee of the church or club that we organized and led for several years, that took so much of our time and energy—why is it so terribly hard to let go of the responsibility, to stand aside with warm encouragement and *no interference* while others try out their ideas?

And these children of ours, long since grown up—once they were completely subject to our control, even on such details as to what they ate and wore, and what time they went to bed. Now these children are mature individuals with children of their own. *It's their turn now* to decide what their children do. Why should we be so outraged if they decide that their children may be permitted or denied privileges that are different from those we used? *It's their turn now.*

Perhaps one of the skills we most need to acquire in old age is the ability to recognize in many different situations that *we've had our turn.*

PART II

Old Age: Its Challenges and Opportunities

6

The Peripheral Position

Do all old people, I wonder, react as I do, with considerable irritation to the sentimental approach to old age? This is no time, it seems to me, for sentimentality, for closing the eyes to facts, for soft-pedaling the realities of existence. On the contrary, it is a time when what is most needed is courage enough to look the facts in the face. Old age frequently means loss of economic status, decreasing physical strength, waning energy, contracting circles of activity, gradual loss of power and influence, increasing ill health, pain, suffering, loneliness, bereavement, and the imminence of death. Quite a list of grim realities to face up to. All three dimensions of life—past, present and future—sometimes seem shrouded in a mist of gloom.

No matter how happy the past may have been, dwelling on it now may produce a deep discontent with the contrasting present. Some of us, moreover, carry a burden of regret for wasted opportunities, for unfulfilled dreams and resolves, for neglected kindness and perhaps for a few deliberate unkindnesses, for callous indifference to the sufferings of others, for failure to respond to human need constantly revealed to us on every side. How desperately we need to repent wholeheartedly, to confess these old sins to our loving Father, to accept His promised forgiveness, and then to put them completely out of our minds, and turn our energies to using our remaining days as God directs!

As for the present, most of us find ourselves in a peripheral position. Loss of power and responsibility is hard to take. People who in their active years were involved in important tasks, feeling the challenge of great opportunities, using their fine creative abilities to solve difficulties and project new undertakings, often find themselves in old (and not so old) age suddenly in the position of observers, looking on from the sidelines, no longer sharing in the power and responsibility of important affairs, their opinions no longer sought, their suggestions brushed aside as unimportant and irrelevant.

No one can deny that this is hard to accept. Not to feel needed is very often fatal to a person's self-esteem. The mother must learn to see as her finest achievement the independence of her child, his maturity proved by his ability to stand on his own without her support. So too, as old age comes on, genuine acceptance of a peripheral position in life is one of the necessities of a wholesome adjustment.

Moreover, once one has achieved this necessary adjustment, it is utterly amazing how many opportunities for valuable contributions to the ongoing life around us are still open to us from the sidelines—opportunities of which we will never be aware if our inward eyes are constantly focused on our difficulties and disadvantages.

So much for the past and the present. What about the future? Suddenly the future has almost ceased to exist. No longer does it stretch endlessly ahead, full of all kinds of challenging opportunities and delightful possibilities. Suddenly it just isn't there—or at least it is so uncertain that the only real certainty is its not too distant termination.

These are the facts—hard, unpleasant, undeniable—that must be faced if we are to live victoriously and triumphantly through these final months and years of life.

It may be helpful to recall that every stage of life, when we were in the midst of it, presented a similar catalogue of gloom part of the time. It is only in retrospect that childhood, and perhaps adolescence, seem carefree and happy. And surely a moment's honest reflection will lead us to admit that in our mature and productive years there were times when we would gladly have shed some of our responsibilities for some much-longed-for leisure.

It seems that each stage of life has its inevitable difficulties and, as surely, its compensations. The protected baby, as safe as human love can make him, still needs to protest and struggle to find himself. The adolescent, surrounded by a supportive family, has to break loose from what seems like unbearable restraint in order to realize his own capabilities. And the mature man or woman, overburdened by responsibilities apparently beyond his strength, perhaps needs that very overload in order, through the struggle, to realize his own potential.

And what about us now, those of us who have developed through all these stages with varying degrees of success? At every preceding stage, struggle has been an integral part of the pattern of our life, bringing with it greater abilities, new strengths, new understandings. But now there is a difference. Struggle against the particular difficulties of old age will get us nowhere. No amount of struggling against physical weakness and lack of energy will make us one whit stronger or more energetic. It will only make our lot harder. Nor will any struggle against the future change it. No resisting the imminence of death is going to postpone it by one second.

In this final stage of our lives, *struggle gets us nowhere*. We have to find a new technique for overcoming our difficulties, a whole new pattern for our lives. I have always loved the comment of Carlyle about the woman who declared, "I accept the universe!" His terse reply was, "Gad! She'd better!"

There is a "word to the wise" for us to take to heart. Just as struggle was the key word in our earlier stages of life, just as it was necessary for our survival and maturation, so there is a key word for our old age: *acceptance*.

Positive acceptance of old age as it is, with no denying of its difficulties, with no shutting of our eyes to any of its undesirable aspects—this is the new technique for us to learn.

"We accept old age!" "Gad! We'd better!" We have no

other choice. Only after acceptance can we go on to discover that in this age, as in all the others, surprising compensations are provided. Only then can we begin to cultivate those gracious skills of living that are peculiarly fitting for old age.

7

Fearfully and Wonderfully Made

I am fearfully and wonderfully made. (Psalm 139:14)

The psalmist who first caught this insight impearled it for the benefit of following generations in these words.

"Fearfully and wonderfully made," indeed! The marvel of our bodies is one most of us take thoughtlessly for granted. Few stop to wonder as the ancient psalmist did. One of the few who did voiced his wonder in a prayer:

Is not sight a jewel? Is not hearing a treasure? Is not speech a glory? O my Lord, pardon my ingratitude, and pity my dullness who am not sensible of these gifts. The freedom of Thy bounty hath deceived me. These things were too near to be considered. Thou presentedst me with Thy blessings, and I was not aware. But now I give thanks and adore and praise Thee for Thine inestimable favors.[1]

Sight, hearing and speech are only three of many marvels in these bodies which we inhabit more or less precariously for a term of years. Think of the steady pulsing of the heart year after year after year. Think of all the complicated processes that take place in the digestive system. Think of the body's amazing healing and recuperative powers. Usually the only time we are aware of any of these miracles is when we complain of their occasional malfunctioning.

My particular favorite among the body miracles is the human hand. What a peculiarly effective instrument it is for carrying out our purposes! How constantly our hands are busy ministering to our own and others' needs, improving our environment, bringing gardens to lovely flowering, giving voices to musical instruments, creating useful and artistic objects! And all these things are accomplished with almost complete unawareness on our part—until we cut a finger, or until the crippling of arthritis suddenly makes us conscious of our loss of dexterity.

Were we creatures without hands, suddenly endowed with them, how we should marvel at their usefulness! Surely such amazing tools should be used sacramentally.

Even arthritic hands need not be despised—they are still capable of sacramental use. I had a dear aunt, who, for years before her death, was constantly knitting for the Red Cross. Literally dozens of sweaters were made by her aged, twisted

---

[1]Thomas Traherne (?1637-1674), in *God of a Hundred Names*, Barbara Greene and Victor Gollancz. (Garden City, New York: Doubleday, 1963).

fingers, and dozens of disaster victims were grateful for her anonymous ministry. And in countless three-generation homes, as in previous centuries, the misshapen hands of the aged still perform almost continuous loving acts of service—washing dishes, mending clothes, comforting the hurts of toddlers.

Nor is this kind of ministry limited to women. Men too have their special abilities to contribute. How many loved toys have come from the home workshops of grandfathers! How many broken toys have been mended! How many articles of furniture have been reconditioned! How many small boys have exclaimed with conviction. "Gosh! Granddad can fix *anything!*"

"Christ has no hands but our hands," sang a poet in a moment of insight. We may be grateful, indeed, that across the world, even with its present weight of woe, hundreds and thousands of hands are dedicated to doing His work today. It is still true that so long as we live and breathe, some portion of that work will remain undone, some bit of God's purpose for some of His creatures will be unfulfilled, unless we, who have passed our years of greatest usefulness, still offer to Him hearts sensitive to the needs of those around us, minds alert to opportunities of possible service, and hands (and tongues) dedicated to the doing of His will.

8

Minor Ecstasies

A tendency to recall the past days can be either a blessing or a curse to us in our later years. If our rememberings are clouded by feelings of guilt, if we dwell on wasted opportunities, on our mistakes and sins, or if we are constantly grieving over past happiness, then our rememberings poison our present living, make it impossible to enjoy present blessings, and spread gloom and unhappiness all around us.

If on the other hand we remember with joyful thanksgiving the days gone by, if we recall the marvelous way God's hand has been upon us, and how He has so frequently brought surprising good out of seeming evil, then our memories can be strengthening to us, and a blessing to those around us.

Elizabeth Gray Vining has described some of the deeply joyous experiences of life as "minor ecstasies." She writes:

Only a few people, and those few but
infrequently, know ecstasy. It is a big word; it
means a state of being outside oneself and outside
time, caught up in an overwhelming emotion; it
implies a high occasion and a greatness of
response to it. Mystics have used the word to
express the ineffable joy of union with Reality, the
flight, in Plotinus' phrase, of the alone to the
Alone; it applies to the selfless raptures of human
love and parenthood, to what artists feel when
what they create seems to be coming through
them from something beyond. With such
grandeur of experience, alps towering over the
plain of daily living, I am not now concerned. I am
thinking of what I have learned to call minor
ecstasies, bits of star dust which are for all of us,
however monotonous our days and cramped our
lives, however limited our opportunities.[1]

"Minor ecstasies" is a happy phrase. Everyone has a few
memories of such moments—brief flickers of intense
joy—gone almost before they are recognized, but so intense
that they remain forever living memories capable of being
recalled instantly, with something of the original magic still
lingering.

I remember one such moment. I was nineteen years old. I
was struggling to regain my balance after a sudden ending to
my first experience of falling in love. Love had always been a

---

[1]*The World in Tune*, Elizabeth Gray Vining. (New York: Harper & Row, 1954), pp.
27-28.

taken-for-granted natural thing to me, and it had not seemed *too* miraculous to be the object of this special kind of love; but then came the totally unexpected ending. Such a pitiful ending. Nothing great or tragic, not the death of the loved one on a battlefield or anything at all dramatic, just the realization on his part that he did not love me after all. My pride and self-esteem were shattered. My world had come tumbling down like a house of cards.

But life went on. And one night a few weeks later, I was walking alone up a country road to the school where I was a resident teacher. As I walked, sunk deep in my misery, I suddenly lifted my head. I saw the outline of the hills against the starry sky, and into my mind flashed the words "I will lift up mine eyes unto the hills, from whence cometh my help. My help cometh from the Lord, which made heaven and earth" (Psalm 121:1-2).

I stood still, transfixed, my face lifted to the sky. And suddenly I knew in the innermost part of my being, that *help had come*. God was there! I knew it beyond any shadow of a doubt. He was flooding my heart with an awareness of His reality and power! God himself had driven away the weight of black depression, and was filling my heart to overflowing with His joy and peace! How long I stood there motionless, under the eternal stars, glorying in this unexpected revelation, I have no idea. Eventually, I walked on up the hill with a glorious assurance of being able to face and cope with anything life might bring, because I had been given the knowledge of the inexhaustible Source of help in time of need.

A minor ecstasy, a bit of star dust, as vivid today in memory as though it had happened only yesterday, instead of sixty-five years ago—far more vivid than the need that called it forth.

Another minor ecstasy comes to mind. I had been away from home for several weeks. I had just alighted from the return plane. As I started down the long passageway from the gate, I caught sight of my family far ahead. At the same minute my three-year-old grandson saw me, broke away from his mother's hand, and came racing down the passageway, shrieking at the top of his lungs, "Gay-Gay! Gay-Gay!" Amused passengers moved aside to give him room, and several turned to see the blessed recipient of such an enthusiastic welcome. I braced myself for his onslaught, and caught him to me with a depth of joy that can truly be described as ecstatic.

Love, the greatest miracle in existence! How often we take it entirely for granted! We do well to accept it humbly, with awe and reverence, and with ecstatic response whenever we are its object.

These minor ecstasies from the past are memories to be recalled frequently and relived. They renew our faith in the goodness of life, strengthen our belief in the possibility of more ecstatic experiences, and increase our ability to recognize and savor them when they occur.

9

Misers of Time

"I can't wait till next week!" "I wish my birthday would hurry up and come!" "How long *now* until Christmas?"

With such heedless prodigality does youth wish away time! Not so with us oldsters. It may be true that we are anticipating something that will happen next week, or next month, or next year. (Seldom do we dare look much beyond that.) But *in the meantime* we treasure the days with miserly thrift.

At long last we have learned fully to appreciate the Sanskrit "Salutation to the Dawn":

> Look well to this day! For it is life.
>   The very life of life.
> In its brief course lie all the verities
> And realities of your existence:
>   The bliss of growth,

The glory of action,
The splendor of beauty:
For yesterday is but a dream,
And tomorrow is only a vision,
But today, well-lived,
Makes every yesterday a dream of happiness,
And every tomorrow a vision of hope.
Look well, therefore, to this day.

Kalidasa (c. 500)

One Christmas I opened a small package and unrolled a cloth calendar, a lovely thing of soft browns, muted reds, and golds, with a Bible verse painted on the cloth: "This is the day which the Lord hath made; we will rejoice and be glad in it" (Psalm 118:24).

"Oh," I exclaimed, "that's one of my favorite Bible verses!"

"I know," said my twelve-year-old granddaughter, nodding her head. "That's why I got it for you. I thought of you the moment I saw it."

The cloth hanging (the calendar long since removed) still adorns the wall of my room, a constant reminder that happiness is not a result of fortuitous circumstances, but is the by-product of a right relationship with God and with our neighbors.

What are the things that prevent us from living happily today? Sometimes present factors are largely responsible for our discontent: physical discomfort, or pain, loneliness, boredom. These need to be overcome by a special effort to change our mood, perhaps by immersing ourselves in some congenial activity, perhaps by a general mental housecleaning that sweeps out the gloomy cobwebs of discontent and allows the cheery thoughts of God's manifest blessings to crowd our minds.

Often, however, in addition to the day's legitimate difficulties, yesterday and tomorrow cast their ugly shadows across what could be the bright gladness of today. Too many of us spend our days in useless repining over happy yesterdays now gone (instead of being grateful for such happy memories) or in dreading the future, worrying about calamities that, often, never happen.

Hannah Whitall Smith tells a pertinent anecdote, reminding us first that there is scriptural authority for this emphasis on living in the present. For we are commanded: "Take therefore no thought for the morrow: for the morrow shall take thought for the things of itself. Sufficient unto the day is the evil thereof" (Matthew 6:34).

She goes on to tell about a poor household drudge, "a woman who earned a precarious living by daily labor, but who was a joyous, triumphant Christian":

"Ah, Nancy," said a gloomy Christian lady to her one day, who almost disapproved of her constant cheerfulness, and yet envied it,—"Ah, Nancy, it is all well enough to be happy now, but I should think the thoughts of your future would sober you. Only suppose, for instance, that you should have a spell of sickness, and be unable to work; or suppose your present employers should move away, and no one else should give you anything to do; or suppose—" "Stop!" cried Nancy, "I never supposes. De Lord's my Shepherd, and I knows I shall not want. And, honey," she added to her gloomy friend, "it's all dem *supposes* as is making you so mis'able. You'd better give dem all up, and just trust de Lord."[1]

The fewer days we have left, the more we should fill them to the brim with the happiness that comes from a right relationship to God and to our neighbors, with a grateful recognition of "minor ecstasies" which have been ours in the past, with an upwelling gratitude for present blessings, and with a peaceful acceptance of whatever lies ahead. "*This* is the day which the Lord hath made; we will rejoice and be glad in it."

---

[1]*The Christian's Secret of a Happy Life*, Hannah Whitall Smith. (Westwood, New Jersey: Fleming H. Revell, 1952), pp. 149-150.

10

Good Company for Myself

A friend of mine in her eighties spent much of her time alone. "Lonely?" she used to reply to inquirers. "Oh, no! I'm very good company for myself." What a tremendously valuable skill of living, the ability to be good company for oneself!

Surely this ability comes, first of all, from a basically wholesome self-regard, a realization of oneself as an interesting and likeable person. A person characterized by feelings of inferiority, a sense of failure, anxiety, and bitterness would find it difficult to achieve such contentment.

The contented older person has usually achieved an optimistic thought trend that finds genuine enjoyment in the uneventful passing days, savors moments of beauty, joyously recalls minor ecstasies from the past, and faces the future serene and unafraid.

In addition to all this, the contented older person is almost invariably a busy person, one who has cultivated many interests and abilities, and fills his days with pleasurable activities. For the years of lessened physical activity, countless and varied opportunities for enjoying "aloneness" are available.

Reading: This stands high on my personal list of devices for overcoming loneliness and boredom. The contracting circles of physical existence are powerless to confine the mind; and one of the compensations of old age is that now we have time to read what we want to, free from the demands of reading almost exclusively in the narrow limits of occupation or profession. Now we can reach out and sample all the rich areas of literature—biography, philosophy, fiction, drama, poetry. How fortunate we are to live in a country where libraries are usually as near and convenient as grocery stores!

And even though sight is dim, and reading difficult, yet there are records!

Records: How about a study of Shakespeare? Readings of his plays by skillful actors are available in many record libraries. More and more records of other books are becoming available. What a blessing for those with impaired vision!

And of course the whole world of music can be brought into the narrow limits of your own room, even a sick room. You have only to make your own selection.

Tapes: One source of enjoyment available to this generation of oldsters is a tape recorder, and a growing list of available cassettes on every conceivable subject. The entire Bible is available on tapes, as well as innumerable and helpful Bible teachings, sacred music, sermons.

Moreover, the recording of personal letters on tapes can add a completely new dimension to correspondence for elderly parents separated by many miles from their children.

A number of years ago, I discovered the rich possibilities in this kind of correspondence. My elder sister, who was close to ninety, and almost blind, lived halfway across the continent from me. Visits were extremely rare. But one birthday I sent her a tape recorder and a recording on tape of my birthday letter to her. She was overjoyed; and that first tape was followed by others: a reading of Thanksgiving passages from the Bible, a reading of some of her favorite poems, and finally a reading of selections from my latest book. Her daughter reported that the tapes were the source of many hours of happy listening in the last years of her life.

Television: This seems less valuable to me than the items previously mentioned because it is so much less flexible and adaptable to personal interests, but as a means of escaping loneliness it has its uses. Certainly the news broadcasts make any feelings of isolation impossible, and isn't it surprising what a feeling of companionship and intimacy (even though one-sided) you develop toward your favorite newscaster?

Letter-writing: This is an excellent device for overcoming loneliness, and an opportunity for us oldsters to chatter to our hearts' content. Few recipients ever complain that letters are too long!

In this mobile age, many of us find ourselves separated from friends and relatives, but distance need not destroy the ties of friendship that have endured for many years.

Most of us look forward to the influx of mail at Christmas time with genuine anticipation. The family letters and photographs, the brief scrawled messages, even the cards with just a signature, all combine to spread a network of friendly ties that gives us a warm sense of manifold relationships.

These friendly greetings, however, need not be limited to Christmas. Each one of us surely knows the joy of the letter from a dearly loved friend that comes unexpectedly and for no apparent reason. We could provide reasons for more frequent contacts.

One helpful device is to set aside a special time each week to be devoted to letter-writing. This is a two-edged technique for combating loneliness, the writing of the letter itself and the delight of receiving an answer.

A Diary: Did you keep a diary when you were an adolescent? I did, and I remember what a safety valve it was for me to be able to confide in it all my innermost wonderings and doubts and feelings, things I would not have told even my best friend. Admittedly, this has its dangers. It *can* be a mere wallowing in self-pity, an indulgence in depressing thoughts. But it may on the contrary be an honest evaluation of the present situation which will result in an awareness of compensations and blessings that have been overlooked, a reminder of our Christian faith, a holding fast to the biblical promises which are the basis for a life of peace under any circumstances.

I recall vividly a personal experience that happened to me several years ago. That particular morning one disturbing thing after another had happened, nothing in itself important, but a number of minor annoyances. I had written a note to "Any Male Saint" and left it on the kitchen table, asking for someone to carry an empty rubbish barrel to the third floor. Apparently each male saint decided someone else would respond. The barrel did not arrive.

The next thing that happened was that I caught a usually cooperative grandson on his way out the door, and asked him to mail a manuscript for me at the post office. And he said, "I'll do it later. I'm on a tight time schedule just now. I'm due at the university for a class."

And so it went! The morning mail brought a disappointing rejection slip from one of the publishers; a disturbing telephone call came from a friend who was ill.

The net result was that when I finally tumbled into bed far later than my usual time, I was feeling distinctly "battered." I slept restlessly, and wakened at my usual early time, feeling the weight of the world on my shoulders.

I got a cup of coffee, and retreated into the library for my quiet time with the Lord, but I had difficulty in lifting myself above the disturbances of yesterday. I knew that I was about to be engulfed by a wave of self-pity.

I was sitting on the couch, staring at a lovely plant of yellow chrysanthemums on the table, and suddenly I sighed and threw my head back against the couch with a feeling of utter discouragement. And as I did so, something odd happened. I was aware that the appearance of the chrysanthemums had changed. Instead of seeing the lovely, perfect flowers on their long stems, what I saw was a confused, shapeless mass of yellow and green. My bifocals were playing tricks on me, distorting out of all recognition the image of the plant.

And it was then that the Lord spoke to my heart: "You are looking at yesterday through spiritual bifocals. You're looking at everything that happened with your self-centered carnal mind. You're focused on yourself, and on how everything that happened affected *you*. And you're seeing everything not *as it is* but as your self-centeredness distorts it!" And I lifted my head and said, "Yes, Lord. You're right."

But He wasn't through with me yet. "Let this mind be in you that was in Christ Jesus," He said. "Get rid of your spiritual bifocals. Get yourself out of the way so that you can discern the truth! No one of these people who hurt your feelings did it on purpose. Each one of them is in need of your understanding, your patience, your forgiveness! Let this mind be in you that was in Christ Jesus."

I picked up my Bible and turned to one of my favorite passages, and read over the familiar words:

Although the fig tree shall not blossom, neither
shall fruit be in the vines; the labour of the olive
shall fail and the fields shall yield no meat; the
flock shall be cut off from the fold, and there shall
be no herd in the stalls: Yet I will rejoice in the
Lord, I will joy in the God of my salvation.
(Habakkuk 3:17-18)

Well, I wasn't concerned about fig trees and grape vines,
and olives, and grain fields, and flocks and herds, but I
surely had my own list of "Althoughs"! On an impulse, I
picked up a notebook and began to write:

Although I am past eighty years old, and my
physical strength and energy are far less than they
once were. . . .
Although I can no longer drive a car, and so I must
depend on the kindness of others. . . .
Although the circles of my activity are narrowing
rapidly. . . .
Although people around me occasionally seem
hasty and inconsiderate and even unaware of the
unavoidable difficulties of old age. . . .

On and on I went listing every "Although" on my list in
detail, facing forthrightly every unpleasant and inescapable
fact. Then I went back to the beginning and started to read
over what I had written. And as I read each "Although," I

suddenly realized that the Lord was revealing to me the particular answer, the "Yet" which His love had provided for each specific "Although," the "Yet" that could enable me to conclude my tale of woe with the very words of Habakkuk: "Yet I will rejoice in the Lord, I will joy in the God of my salvation"!

Over eighty I surely am, *yet* I am in remarkably good physical health. Dependent on the family, yes, indeed, *yet* such a dear, loving family! Somewhat confined and limited because I no longer drive, *yet* living in such a delightful home, with transportation easily arranged whenever necessary. Narrowing circles of activity, of course, *yet* with the joy of my writing continuing and even deepening with the passing years.

And on and on, and on, to the very end of the list. And once more I turned to Habakkuk:

> Yet I will rejoice in the Lord, I will joy in the God of my salvation. The Lord God is my strength, and he will make my feet like hinds' feet, and he will make me to walk upon mine high places. (Habakkuk 3:18-19)

And so at last I was able to give God genuine thanks that He *had* made my feet like hinds' feet, and enabled me to climb out of despondency into the joyous freedom of my high places.

Solitaire and Puzzles: "Do *you* play solitaire?" my friends sometimes ask in surprise. And I am almost hesitant to admit that I find solitaire at times a completely satisfactory substitute for a table of bridge. I am far less likely to be annoyed by myself, than by the stupidities and irritating habits of many card players I have known! And it is easier to stop when I've had enough.

Another of my favorite relaxations is doing puzzles. I like them all, crossword, crypto-quotes, even jigsaws.

Occupational Therapy: When I was growing up, few people, I think, had even heard of "occupational therapy," but my mother knew all about the danger of Satan's finding mischief for idle hands, and so we girls acquired a number of skills for which I have always been exceedingly grateful. My mother was an expert needlewoman, and we were introduced at various times to many forms of sewing, hemstitching, featherstitching, smocking, embroidery, to knitting, crocheting, beadwork, rugmaking (braided and hooked), and even to leather work and woodburning. So we learned early the joy of creative arts and crafts.

Nowadays the psychological value of such occupations is widely recognized, and men as well as women find enjoyment in painting, clay modeling, copper tooling, and similar pastimes.

Service Activities: Occupations that are tied in with some form of service to others have an additional element of enjoyment. These help to overcome loneliness by establishing ties (anonymous but real) with the needy ones of the world. Do you remember how during the war, groups of women found deep and genuine satisfaction and fulfillment in folding bandages and knitting for the Red Cross? Something of the same satisfaction is available even to the shut-in, who finds, perhaps in connection with her church's mission program, some project which can make good use of her time and abilities, knitting afghans or baby blankets, or making bandages for lepers, for example.

Surely with so many opportunities for happy, worthwhile occupations each of us should be able to find the acitivities which may enable us to declare: "Lonely? Oh, no! I'm very good company for myself." Amen and Amen.

11

Look for a Lovely Thing

To my father I owe an awareness of beauty that is one of the indestructible pleasures of living. Old age is powerless to eradicate it. Even fading eyesight cannot totally deprive me, for there is always memory.

Sara Teasdale has given inspired expression to the value of remembered beauty:

> Oh, better than the minting
> Of a gold-crowned king
> Is the safe-kept memory
> Of a lovely thing.[1]

Three memories of lovely things stand out from my early days of childhood, all three associated with my father.

The earliest one dates from the time when I was perhaps

---

[1]"The Coin," in *Stars Tonight* (New York: Macmillan, 1930)

four years old. I was lying half awake one morning in early spring. Suddenly my father was bending over me.

"I want to show you something," he said, and lifting me in his strong arms he carried me to a window in another room. "Look!" he said. "Look at the pear tree!"

In wonder I gazed at the tree. The early rays of sunlight flashed upon living bits of color all over its branches. A whole flock of migrating warblers had paused in their long flight and had been our unexpected overnight guests. And to the jewel-like beauty of the tiny feathered forms was added the loveliness of their morning songs of praise.

Breathless, we watched and listened, until as though at a given signal, the flock whirred aloft and winged their way southward.

The second incident also happened in the early morning. This time it was a glorious sunrise that I was lifted from my bed to enjoy. The sky, from the eastern horizon to the zenith, was covered with fluffy, small gray clouds, and each one was edged with vivid crimson.

The third memory is of a time when my father and I were walking along the Jersey seashore. It was low tide, and the mighty ocean that had been huge, raging billows a few hours earlier was now almost as still as a lake. Small lazy waves, scarcely more than ripples, rolled up across the sand and flowed gently back again, leaving the wet sand smooth and firm beneath our bare feet. And then, as one wave receded, the sand was suddenly alive with hundreds of little living sea creatures, each no more than half an inch long and a quarter of an inch wide, enclosed in two tiny "sunrise" shells, shells of pale pink, pale yellow, pale lavender, rayed like the radiant morning sky, each one lovelier than the last, a glory of exquisite miniature creations. What could one do but stand still and think of the wonders of God?

Sensitivity to beauty in its myriad forms is one blessing old age cannot take from us. Sara Teasdale's advice in the following brief poem is good for anyone, but is especially appropriate for us oldsters:

> Stars over snow,
>   And in the west a planet
> Swinging below a star—
>   Look for a lovely thing and you will find it,
> It is not far
>   It never will be far.[2]

Should we cultivate this sensitivity to beauty merely because of the aesthetic enjoyment it provides? Surely there is a deeper reason. Such moments bring us close to the mystery at the center of life.

> There is an hour of the Indian night, a little before the first glimmer of dawn, when the stars are unbelievably clear and close above, shining with a radiance beyond our belief in this foggy land. The trees stand silent around one with a friendly presence. As yet there is no sound from awakening birds; but the whole world seems to be intent, alive, listening, eager. At such a moment

---

[2]"Night," *ibid.*

the veil between the things that are seen and the things that are unseen becomes so thin as to interpose scarcely any barrier at all between the eternal beauty and truth and the soul which would comprehend them.[3]

---

[3]*The Light of Christ*, J.S. Hoyland (London: George Allen & Unwin, 1928.)

PART III

Three-Generation Homes

12

Living Together

In spite of the fact that three-generation homes are frowned on by sociologists, they still exist, not so universally as in the years before the establishment of social security and the prevalence of nursing homes and centers for aging citizens, but still in appreciable numbers.

A young social worker of my acquaintance tells with great glee of a conversation she had with her supervisor in a family agency. The supervisor took exception to a plan the social worker had proposed for one family which involved a three-generation home.

"What's wrong with having grandparents in the home?" asked the social worker a bit belligerently. "We often had a grandparent with us, sometimes two at a time. One of my grandmothers was confined to her bed for the last two years of her life, but I don't remember it as anything but a positive experience."

The supervisor stared at her unbelievingly. Then she remarked tartly, "Well, all I can say is, your mother must have been a remarkable woman!"

As for me, I have lived happily in three different three-generation homes, the first in my childhood, the second when my own family was growing up, and the third now in my old age with my daughter's family.

There are, of course, many families and situations where three generations could not live happily together. Some old people seem to develop extraordinary skill in being completely unlovable and irritating. Judgmental, complaining, easily offended, self-centered, they seem to acquire a sense of status and importance in direct proportion to the amount of trouble they stir up. On the other hand, some young people are inconsiderate, resentful of criticism, opinionated, impatient of any interference, insensitive to the feelings of those around them, short-tempered, and basically unloving.

It seems obvious that people with these personality traits, young and old, cannot live happily together. Neither, incidentally, can they live happily apart. They simply cannot live happily—period.

Whenever I think of the difficulties involved in three-generation homes, I chuckle, remembering an incident that occurred several years ago in a family camp. A group of young parents were discussing family relationships, and someone mentioned the question of three-generation homes. The leader had all the answers. He echoed the opinion of those sociologists who condemn such arrangements as completely inadvisable. In the midst of his tirade he suddenly became aware that my daughter and I (who live together in this impossible situation) were listening with amusement. He stopped short, embarrassed, but my daughter rose to the occasion.

"You're quite right," she commented, pleasantly. "Having grandparents in the home does create a number of difficult problems." She paused a moment, and then added quietly, "*So does having children.* But no one suggests that we should stop having children because of the problems."

Given the willingness of all involved to find solutions for the problems that arise, a generous amount of love and forgiveness on both sides, a desire and a willingness to be useful according to their capabilities on the part of the grandparents, and genuine gratitude on the part of the young parents for services rendered, the chances are good that a three-generation home will succeed surprisingly well in meeting the needs of all its various members.

13

The Children's People

How many times I recall with warm and tender amusement something that happened years ago, when my now married granddaughter was a three-year-old!

She had been teasing her busy mother to read a book to her, and her mother said, "Oh, go and ask Gay-Gay. She'll read to you."

So I put aside my knitting, and the toddler and I curled up in a big chair and read the book. When we finished, the child drew a long, satisfied breath and trotted back to her mother, to whom she announced gravely and happily, "Gay-Gay and Grandpa are *the children's people.*"

What an accolade! And what blessed grandparents to be so regarded! But this delightful relationship can be established and maintained only if the grandparents genuinely accept the peripheral position, only if they can happily admit that the responsibility of training the children is first and always the *parents'!*

No two generations of parents ever raise the children in the same way. When grandparents in the home seek to impose *their* rules and *their* regulations on the children, the results are inevitable: rebellion from the children, resentment from the parents, and hurt feelings from the oldsters.

The wise (but difficult to achieve) attitude is to be always responsive to opportunities to be useful, to enrich the children's lives, to take some of the twenty-four-hour daily load from the parents, but never to assume responsibility for the children's discipline.

The most helpful contribution a grandparent can make to a troubled family situation, when parents and children are temporarily at loggerheads, is to take himself entirely out of it. Every extra person in such a family crisis adds confusion and irritation. If circumstances make physical withdrawal impossible (as, for instance, if the family is all together in the car) there is still possible *the gift of silence.* Adding two cents worth of advice to reinforce the parent is both unnecessary and unwise. It invites answering back on the part of the children, and distracts their attention from their parents.

Happy is the family to which the old people contribute their gift of silence at the appropriate time!

> There is one who keeps silent because
>   he has no answer,
> While another keeps silent because
>   he knows when to speak. (Ecclesiasticus 20:6)

14

"Guest" Grandparents

I remember with great joy and tenderness an older couple who often had a meal with us in our home when my three children were growing up.

Our entertaining was always completely informal, family style. Our guests, to quote my husband, "took us as we were." "What's good enough for us is good enough for our friends," he used to say.

The Thompsons had been friends of my family for many years. Mr. Thompson had been before his retirement the principal of the little public school which my sisters and I attended, so that he had known me from my kindergarten days. Mrs. Thompson, too, was a friend of long standing. She had been active for years in our Sunday school and had occasionally substituted in the public school.

We often had other dinner guests, of course, but the Thompsons stand out in my memory above all others because of the effect they had on our children. Here were two guests that the children enjoyed as much as we did.

"The Thompsons coming to dinner? Oh, goody!" was the invariable reaction. And because of the children's attitude, I was always relaxed and easy.

After dinner, when the children had been packed off to bed, the four of us grown-ups would settle down to a happy time of friendly talk.

"Florence," one or the other of our guests would be sure to say, "you *do* have the most charming children."

And I would answer a bit ruefully, "Yes, they were charming tonight. They always are, when you are here. But you should see them sometimes!"

Over the years I have thought frequently about the Thompsons, and have wondered what it was in their approach that brought out the best and most lovable side of my three children, who were, as I very well knew, capable sometimes of displaying most unlovable behavior.

Part of the secret, I am sure, was in a basic attitude of acceptance, approval, and pleasant expectation. The Thompsons were completely at ease with the children. They both had a direct approach on a man-to-man basis, without affectation or condescension. They were genuinely interested in what the children had to say, and showed that interest by giving undivided attention to them when they spoke. They courteously included the children in their conversation, sometimes stopping to give them a special word of explanation. Their whole attitude and every remark they made showed their respect for the children *as persons*.

Since I have been a grandparent-in-the-home, I have often wished that I could exert the same beneficent influence that the Thompsons exerted in our home. This was easier to achieve in the days when we were truly house guests, when these visits were a rarity, rose-colored days of family reunion passing all too quickly.

As a member of the family, however, it has become evident to me that there is still the need for the same attitudes that make a successful guest.

Pleasant guests are always outspoken in their appreciation of the hosts' efforts to make them comfortable. Grandparents in the home would do well to make the expression of such appreciation a habit, and not to fall into the attitude of taking all the love and concern for granted.

Understanding guests always build up and reinforce the parents' faith in the genuine lovableness of their children. "Guest" grandparents can serve a high purpose here. When the parents are troubled by a child's discourtesy or misbehavior, what they do *not* need is a sympathetic, "Oh, isn't he exasperating! I don't know how you stand it!"

On the contrary, what they really need is reassurance. "Oh, you know this isn't really like him! Usually he's reasonable and more thoughtful." Or maybe, "What do you expect of a child his age? This is completely typical behavior. It's a part of growing up." Or maybe even a gentle reminder: "What he needs is just an extra dose of loving. The more unlovable he seems, the more he needs it."

Welcome guests are almost always good listeners. No overworked mother ever has time to listen with undivided attention to all the conversational efforts of all the children all the time. A grandparent, determined to be a courteous "guest," can often be a good substitute listener. But will the children accept the grandparents in the role of listener? Only, I feel sure, if the listening grows out of genuine interest; only if the listening is wholehearted, and not just an impatient waiting for an opportunity to take over the conversation.

No parent can always be available for reading out loud. A "guest" grandparent, however, can be ready to insert a quiet and relaxing "book time" at appropriate intervals between the periods of normal, noisy activity.

No parent has enough time to entertain sick children during the slow days of convalescence, or bored children on stormy days when the usual occupations lose their charm. A "guest" grandparent who develops a mild passion for games (checkers, dominoes, anagrams, parcheesi, chess, etc.) may build a relationship with grandchildren that leads to hours of happy companionship through the years, and may incidentally be instrumental in helping children to achieve the joy of playing, regardless of victory or defeat.

The idea of being a "guest" grandparent leads to a difficult to achieve, but highly desirable, attitude, a certain degree of detachment. No guest worthy of the name would ever interfere or become involved in family problems or difficulties, and a "guest" grandparent does well to withdraw to his own room when these inevitable rough spots occur.

The member-of-the-family grandparent who finds it easier to adjust by thinking of himself as a permanent guest may discover the paradoxical truth that to the family he soon ceases to be a guest, and becomes an accepted and full-fledged member of the group. The more he successfully manages to maintain in his own mind his status as a guest, the more easily and naturally the family accepts him as a loved and welcome member of the fellowship.

15

Talking and Listening

Why is it that as we grow old, the tendency to chatter becomes well nigh irresistible? My grandmother, crippled by a broken hip that never healed properly, was for a number of years confined to her room, moving from her bed only with great difficulty to a specially padded arm chair. She had a sunny disposition, and bore considerable pain with amazing patience and fortitude. And how she loved to talk! Visitors were her chief enjoyment in life.

One of her friends was urging her teen-age son to drop in for a visit once in a while. "But I don't know what to talk about!" he objected.

"Talk?" replied his mother. "You won't need to talk. All you'll have to do is listen!"

How truly that might be said of many of us! What a tendency we have to run on and on, to add story to story, to hurry to hold our audience with such remarks as "And that reminds me . . ." or "Another time . . ." or "But I haven't told you yet . . ."!

Is this due to the inevitable loneliness of older people? One of the results of the peripheral position is often a feeling of isolation, and perhaps out of this comes the urgency to grasp and hold the center of attention whenever possible, to rebuild our sense of our own importance, to know again the feeling of being listened to with respect.

Unfortunately, too often the results are the opposite of those desired. The chattering older person gets to be a bore, and worsens the very isolation against which he is struggling.

There seems to be only one cure for this situation, and it is a difficult one to apply. It is the cultivation of the art of being a good listener. This requires, I think, a genuine acceptance of the peripheral position, and a determined transfer of attention from self-centered concerns to the interests of others. Loneliness can be overcome better by relating oneself to others through a real interest in *their* doings and feelings than by determinedly projecting one's own ideas and emotions into the relationship. A good listener is rarely lonely.

In every troubled family situation, moreover, a good listener may prove a healing influence. He may provide a sympathetic, nonjudgmental sounding board, capable of absorbing poured-out feelings of exasperation and frustration, and thus provide a safety valve for the release of tension. Every family should have at least one good listener!

And now what about the "good talker"? Here we are not

going to be concerned about the usual definition: "one who says interesting things in an interesting way." We are going to make up our own definition: A good talker is one whose talking is good for the family situation!

For years I have loved the description of the power of the tongue from the Epistle of James:

> If any man offend not in word, the same is a perfect man, and able also to bridle the whole body. Behold, we put bits in the horses' mouths, that they may obey us; and we turn about their whole body. Behold also the ships, which though they be so great, and are driven of fierce winds, yet are they turned about with a very small helm, withersoever the governor listeth. Even so the tongue is a little member, and boasteth great things. Behold, how great a matter a little fire kindleth! For every kind of beasts, and of birds, and of serpents, and of things in the sea, is tamed, and hath been tamed of mankind: But the tongue can no man tame; it is an unruly evil, full of deadly poison. (James 3:2-5, 7, 8)

We are thinking here of a "good" talker as one who is constantly trying to control his unruly tongue, who recognizes its potential for spreading poison, and also its potential for healing. Deliberately, with conscious determination, he seeks to use this peculiarly powerful instrument for the good of family life.

Do you remember the fairy story "Toads and Diamonds"? The beautiful and unappreciated maiden goes to the well to fetch water, and is accosted by a poor old woman (a good fairy in disguise), who asks her for a drink of water. The maiden complies graciously, and because of her kindness is given a gift: from then on at every word she speaks a jewel will drop from her lips. Upon her return home, her amazed and delighted stepmother hastens to send her own ill-tempered daughter to the well, hoping that she, too, may be the recipient of such amazing good fortune. But the girl finds no poor old woman at the well. Instead, a proud and imperious princess demands a drink. The girl answers insolently, and *her* reward is that from then on, at every word she speaks, toads and vipers fall from her lips.

Toads and diamonds! What a deep truth is hidden in this pictorial tale, and surely it is a truth especially needed by those of us with three-quarters of a century of living behind us. Too many of us, as we grow older, become tart and bitter, and complaining; whining words spread their ugliness all around us. Few of us have the grace to guard our lips so that consideration for others, gratitude, appreciation, and love fill our surroundings with spiritual treasure and scatter everywhere the subtle fragrance of loving kindness.

16

Mealtimes

At no time perhaps in the twenty-four hours of the day is the difference in child training between the generations more noticeable than at mealtimes.

Who now, for instance, would dream of expecting a modern child to speak only when he's spoken to? Or who would correct an overly talkative youngster at the dinner table with the reminder that children should be seen and not heard? Those days, for good or bad, are gone forever.

For many grandparents, however, the echo of such restrictions still lingers in their consciousness from their childhood days and, to a lesser degree, from the days when their children were growing up.

Something in some old people's make-up reacts with voluble chatter to the relaxation of a good meal and a more or less captive audience. Food also relaxes children's tongues, and sometimes the insistent competition for a tired mother's attention causes tension and irritability. Few of us oldsters have learned the skill of sandwiching in brief comments that form no real interruption to the family chatter. Usually when a grandparent speaks, there seems to be an expectation, almost, indeed, a demand, that all other conversation stop; and many meals could easily be dominated by a continuous monologue. It is revealing to be aware of our own reaction to a child's interruption of an adult conversation. Most of us resent it, and are apt to show our resentment in subtle (and not so subtle) ways.

To be aware of this mealtime problem is to be part way to a solution. Tactful grandparents will consciously accept their role as onlookers at the family table, will firmly limit their table conversation to brief comments that do not carry with them a whole train of attached incidents, will try to earn the reputation of being good listeners, and will accept without resentment inattention and interruptions.

It is even possible that, recognizing the difficulties, grandparents might prefer to have most of their meals apart from the rest of the family. A rare grandparent might earn the gratitude of a harassed mother by suggesting this arrangement himself: "Look, let me have a tray in my room (or out on the porch, or in the library); I'm in the middle of a chapter I'd like to finish," or "I'm tired, and I'd like to be quiet."

Sometimes in homes where this procedure has been worked out, the grandparent becomes a specially invited guest for a birthday meal. Sometimes too, one of the grandchildren will demand: "I want my dinner on a tray too.

I'll eat with grandfather tonight."

Do you remember the old fable of the narrow-necked jar? The more of its contents the inserted hand tried to grasp, the more difficult it was to withdraw the hand. There is a parallel here: Grandparents who are grasping and demanding defeat their own purposes and increase their loneliness and bitterness. When they cease demanding, and remain pleasantly but responsively aloof, much of what they really want comes to them without any effort on their part.

P.S. If I were writing to parents instead of to grandparents, I might be inclined to make a different emphasis.

A few years ago I was walking with my six-year-old grandson through a field of goldenrod, following a rough path almost completely overgrown. The path led downhill, and the going was fairly difficult. Suddenly I stepped in a hole and sat down in an ungraceful heap.

"Are you all right?" asked Ted, anxiously.

And when I assured him I was not hurt, he held out his hand to help me to my feet. And for the rest of the walk he showed a new awareness of my limitations.

"Be careful, Gay-Gay," he cautioned. "There's a big stone here." And "Watch out for the briers." And "Here's a log across the path. Can you step over it?"

I should like to remind parents that exposure to the feebleness and the idiosyncrasies of old age is obviously the only way young people can develop that consideration and courtesy toward elderly people which is so charming. The presence of grandparents in the home is a priceless opportunity to develop in children the very understandings and responses which will add blessedness to the years ahead (and not so far ahead at that), when the parents themselves will be "the old people."

Children who have been trained to affectionate tolerance for the foibles of their grandparents are far more apt to prove understanding and accepting of their own parents in their declining years.

PART IV

A Faith for Old Age

17

Sustaining Faith

Some time ago there appeared in the *Reader's Digest* the following account of a true incident:

> A neighbor in my Indiana home town has grown old more sweetly than anyone I've ever known. Wishing to know the secret of her poise and contentment, I said to her, "I've wondered how it feels to be eighty-five years old."
>
> Her face lighted up as she replied, "Oh, it's just like Saturday afternoon on the farm, when the work is all done and you're ready for Sunday."[1]

What contentment and acceptance and deep, sustaining faith are reflected in those words! How one might envy that blessed octogenarian the faith that was so obviously a source of sustenance and spiritual strength in the declining years of life!

[1] Mrs. Daniel W. Boyer, "Life in These United States," *Reader's Digest* (March, 1967), p. 77

Nor is that woman a lone example, for serenely contented elderly people are to be met often. Every Christian church has its shining examples of these gentle saints who have obviously accepted old age and all its discomforts and liabilities with a triumphant and gracious serenity that bears witness to the rich sufficiency of their faith.

What a pity that so many of us fight the idea of old age, resist it in spite of its inevitability, and poison the last years of living with vain regrets and bitter resentment! Why do we not instead make our own those tremendous affirmations of the Christian faith which have proved their value through generation after generation of tumultuous, tempest-torn living, those truths by which countless thousands of ordinary persons have lived triumphantly through all the vicissitudes of life and have faced the mystery of death and the hereafter serene and confident?

No two people would choose exactly the same affirmations or would express them in the same way. Each will have his unique creed, the result of his individual experience. Some of the affirmations, however, in some form, would surely appear in any statement of Christian belief. For what they may be worth, the following chapters present a few of the particular affirmations upon which my faith rests.

18

Thou Art My God!

These four words are frequently repeated in the Bible, four words of tremendous significance.

> Thou art my God, and I will praise thee: thou art my God, I will exalt thee. (Psalm 118:28)

> I trusted in thee, O Lord: I said, Thou art my God. My times are in thy hand. . . . O how great is thy goodness, which thou has laid up for them that fear thee, which thou hast wrought for them that trust in thee before the sons of men! Thou shalt hide them in the secret of thy presence from the pride of man: thou shalt keep them secretly in a pavilion from the strife of tongues. (Psalm 31:14-15, 19-20)

Thou art my God! Thou—the personal pronoun implies a Person—a Being capable of personal relationships: a "Thou" whom I can know, and who knows me. No impersonal "Creative Force," or "Ground of Our Being" is capable of loving and of being loved. But the Bible asserts that "we love him because he first loved us" (1 John 4:19). He—not It: Thou.

Art—Thou *art*. Our hearts and minds cry out for reality. God is the ultimate Reality—no figment of our imagination, no unreal result of wishful thinking. Reality. A Reality that can be experienced. "In the beginning, God . . ." (Genesis 1:1). "Which is, and which was, and which is to come, the Almighty" (Revelation 1:8).

My—Thou art *my* God. No God, however powerful, however awe-inspiring, can draw me to Him and awaken in my heart belief and trust and devotion, unless I *know* by my experience of Him that He is aware of me as I am of Him. He must be *my* God.

God—Thou art my *God*—the ultimate Reality of my life: the giver of life and death and eternal life: the Source of every good desire, the satisfaction of every need. *Thou—art—my—God!*[1]

If you find that it is impossible for you to make this affirmation honestly, do not despair. The Bible has innumerable promises for you to take to heart. Study them until they become a part of your language of worship, to be called to mind whenever you need them. The first selection below is a part of David's charge to his son, Solomon:

Know thou the God of thy father, and serve him

[1] From *Thou Art My God*, Florence M. Taylor

with a perfect heart and with a willing mind: for the Lord searcheth all hearts, and understandeth all the imaginations of the thoughts: if thou seek him, he will be found of thee. (1 Chronicles 28:9)

Hast thou now known? hast thou not heard, that the everlasting God, the Lord, the Creator of the ends of the earth, fainteth not, neither is weary? there is no searching of his understanding. He giveth power to the faint; and to them that have no might he increaseth strength. They that wait upon the Lord shall renew their strength; they shall mount up with wings as eagles; they shall run and not be weary; and they shall walk and not faint. (Isaiah 40:28-29, 31)

Ye shall seek me, and find me, when ye shall search for me with all your heart. (Jeremiah 29:13)

Thou art my God! This is the one basic affirmation upon which rests the whole structure of our faith. We could almost stop there—so many of the other affirmations are correlative to this one. Thou art my God! I can rest in that assurance.

19

Thou Art the Christ

When Jesus came into the coasts of
Caesarea-Philippi, he asked his disciples, saying,
Whom do men say that I the Son of man am? And
they said, Some say that thou art John the Baptist:
some, Elias; and others, Jeremias, or one of the
prophets. He saith unto them, But whom say ye
that I am? And Simon Peter answered and said,
Thou art the Christ, the Son of the living God.
And Jesus answered and said unto him, Blessed
art thou, Simon Barjona: for flesh and blood hath
not revealed it unto thee, but my Father which is
in heaven. (Matthew 16:13-17)

Thou art the Christ! Other faiths have believed in God,
but only the Christian faith defines that belief in terms of
Christ. The God who is, the God who is the foundation of our

faith, is identified as ". . . the Father of our Lord Jesus Christ, the Father of mercies, and the God of all comfort" (2 Corinthians 1:3).

He is God as interpreted to us by the life and teaching of Jesus. He is the forgiving Father of the parable of the prodigal son (Luke 15:11-32). He is the shepherd seeking the lost and wandering sheep (Luke 15:4-7). He is the constant Companion: "Lo, I am with you alway" (Matthew 28:20). He is the one who claims our complete loyalty and dedication. "Thou shalt love the Lord thy God with all thy heart, and with all thy soul, and with all thy mind" (Matthew 22:37).

Thou art the Christ! The complete revelation of the Father God. "Jesus saith . . . he that hath seen me hath seen the Father" (John 14:9).

Thou art the Christ. In Philippians Paul wrote a moving description of what it means to make this affirmation:

> Let Christ Jesus be your example as to what your attitude should be. For he, who had always been God by nature, did not cling to his prerogatives as God's equal, but stripped himself of all privilege by consenting to be a slave by nature and being born as mortal man. And having become man, he humbled himself by living a life of utter obedience, even to the extent of dying, *and the death he died was the death of a common criminal.* That is why God has now lifted him so high, and has given him the name beyond all names, so that

at the name of Jesus "every knee shall bow", whether in Heaven or earth or under the earth. And that is why, in the end, "every tongue shall confess" that Jesus Christ is the Lord, to the glory of God the Father. (Philippians 2:5-11)[1]

Thou, Jesus, art the Christ, the Son of the living God, my personal Savior, my Redeemer, my resurrected living Lord.

> Jesus Christ is Saviour primarily because He brings God and man together in a fellowship of love. This experience, properly understood, affects life in all its aspects: it has had an incalculable influence on civilization. The saving work of Christ has brought a new conception of personality and of its rich possibilities. . . . It has created in the world a new social sense. . . . He came into the world expressly to save it; he could save it because he was the Son of God in the flesh; and the root and center of salvation is a "personal experience" which in its turn is the promise of both that perfect conformity to the will of God which is the purpose of man's existence, and of that relation to other men which is essential to the realization of the family of God.[2]

---

[1]*The New Testament in Modern English*, Translated by J.B. Phillips (New York: The Macmillan Company, 1963.)

[2]*Harper's Bible Dictionary*, Madeleine S. Miller and J. Lane Miller, in consultation with eminent authorities. (New York: Harper & Brothers, 1952, 1954.)

20

My Body Is the Temple of the Holy Ghost

The Christian faith in a triune God requires the recognition of the third member of the Trinity, the Holy Spirit. "Know ye not," Paul queried the Corinthians, "that your body is the temple of the Holy Ghost?" (1 Corinthians 6:19).

God indwelling man! What a stupendous, breath-taking insight! God within each one of us! God unrecognized, unknown, waiting for our maturing knowledge of Him! God *drawing,* but never coercing us!

> Yea, I have loved thee with an everlasting love:
> therefore with lovingkindness have I drawn thee.
> (Jeremiah 31:3)

God within us! Giving us an innate recognition of good and evil. God, who has placed in the seed the ability to strive upward toward the light and the air, has also placed deep in our hearts the urge to seek Him, to strive for a recognition of His truth, His peace, His joy!

How truly St. Augustine spoke when he said, "Thou hast made us for Thyself, and our hearts are restless till they find their rest in Thee!"

And when we yield to God's constant drawing and gentle pressure, when we open our hearts to receive His Son Jesus as our Savior and Redeemer, then Jesus offers us His final gift, and, for our asking, "baptizes us with fire," filling us to overflowing with His Holy Spirit, granting us inconceivable power to be and to do what God wills for us.

John the Baptist promised this baptism in the Holy Spirit:

> I indeed baptize you with water unto repentance: but he that cometh after me is mightier than I, whose shoes I am not worthy to bear: he shall baptize you with the Holy Ghost, and with fire. (Matthew 3:11)

Jesus made the same promise to His disciples. In His final talk with them before His crucifixion, He said:

> I will pray the Father, and he shall give you another Comforter, that he may abide with you for ever. But the Comforter, which is the Holy Ghost, whom the Father will send in my name, he shall teach you all things, and bring all things to your remembrance, whatsoever I have said unto

you. Peace I leave with you, my peace I give unto you: not as the world giveth, give I unto you. Let not your heart be troubled, neither let it be afraid. (John 14:16, 26-27)

These promises were fulfilled on the day of Pentecost, as recorded in Acts 2. Moreover these same promises are available to us today, as Peter clearly stated in his sermon on that day:

Repent, and be baptized every one of you in the name of Jesus Christ for the remission of sins, and ye shall receive the gift of the Holy Ghost. For the promise is unto you, and to your children, and to all that are afar off, even as many as the Lord our God shall call. (Acts 2:38-39)

21

I Am My Brother's Keeper

Christianity gives no uncertain answer to the age-old question, "Am I my brother's keeper?" (Genesis 4:9). Cain asked it, apparently being convinced that the answer would be, "No, of course not!"

It is a long way from that point of view to Jesus' emphasis on the second great commandment, "Thou shalt love thy neighbour as thyself" (Matthew 22:39); and also to the declaration of the Righteous Judge in His parable of the Last Judgment:

> For I was an hungred, and ye gave me no meat: I was thirsty, and ye gave me no drink: I was a stranger, and ye took me not in: naked, and ye clothed me not: sick, and in prison, and ye visited me not. Verily, I say unto you, Inasmuch as ye did it not to one of the least of these, ye did it not to me. (Matthew 25:42-43, 45)

Admittedly, opportunities for service to others seem to decrease in advancing years, but perhaps that is only an illusion. In God's economy, if we could truly understand it, perhaps the richest and to Him most precious sacrificial service may be reserved for those in the final stages of life's mysterious pilgrimage.

Everyone needs to be useful. But men's ways of evaluating usefulness are undoubtedly vastly different from God's ways. Useful, for what? That question probes the depths of your whole philosophy of life. You cannot answer it adequately without facing the meaning of life itself.

Our age is witnessing innumerable instances of tragic loss of life. Violence and bloodshed in Vietnam, and other trouble spots, thousands of young lives snuffed out. Starvation in India and many other countries, children dying before they have had a chance to live. Racism in Africa—and in America! Legalized abortion on demand! Increase in families broken by divorce, in young people caught in drug addiction, and alcoholism! The list is endless. What a sorry mess the world is in! What is the use of it all?

Faith, the *Christian* faith, declares, in contradiction to this seeming futility, that life *has* purpose, dimly sensed, almost hidden from the searching souls of men, but indubitably woven into the fabric of life itself.

Suppose that part of God's purpose is the creation of human souls made in His image, capable of entering into the world's suffering, and injecting into it the only possible redemptive force—love.

How could such a purpose be fulfilled without those who

suffer? If there were no illness, no weakness, no suffering, no helplessness, how could human beings ever learn helpfulness, sympathy, compassion, self-sacrificing love?

Useful—in the final years of inactivity? Useful—in weeks and months of illness? Useful—when failing sight and hearing make you a burden to others? Useful—when all you have to look forward to is death?

Yes, an unequivocal yes to all these questions. God can use every dedicated soul for His eternal purposes, no matter how erroneously men's judgment declares its uselessness. All that is necessary is the willingness to be used, and the spiritual sensitivity that enables you to hear God's voice speaking in your heart.

A dear Scottish grandmother I knew used to tell of one such dedicated soul: "One day I went to see Ann. She was very ill indeed, quite near the end of a long battle with tuberculosis, but she was cheerful and relaxed. Wracked by fits of coughing, she squeezed my hand in welcome. 'Ah, Libby,' she said, after one specially violent paroxysm of coughing, 'when I was young, I ran here and there at the Lord's bidding, and now He says to me, "Ann! Lie there and cough!" And so—I lie here—and cough.' "

Most of us understandably dread long, drawn-out illnesses, not so much, perhaps, because of the possible suffering involved for ourselves as because of the dread of being a burden on those we love.

But what if this burden, lovingly borne, may be the very means through which these loved ones grow in patience, in spiritual strength, in divine compassion? What if the example of helplessness and suffering, bravely and cheerfully endured, may be exactly what is needed to bring new depths of understanding and new challenges to courageous living to those who stand by?

Who can fathom the mysteries of the interactions of human relationships? How often do we echo the poet's thought:

> God works in a mysterious way
> His wonders to perform.

Milton in his blindness caught a clear insight when he declared: "They also serve, who only stand and wait."

For God's eternal purposes, no dedicated soul is ever useless. One of the insights that come with the passing years is that few satisfactions in life can compare with the awareness of having been instrumental in meeting some human need. When as Christians we follow the commandment to love others as ourselves, the resultant joy is one of the deep and rewarding satisfactions of life.

The toddler who cheerfully picks up his toys and finds himself caught up in a warm hug and hears an enthusiastic "Thank you, darling. That's a real help!" is beginning to learn this important lesson.

The older child, helping with household chores, running errands, baby-sitting with a younger child, needs to hear over and over again, "Oh, thank you, dear. Whatever would I do without such a helpful big sister in the family?"

And the teenager, entering into family consultations,

accepting some necessary sacrifice because of limited financial means or giving up some long-awaited treat because of a family emergency, has earned the right to warm praise and appreciation: "I *knew* we could depend on you!"

All these early experiences are important preparations for adult life. The young couple just starting their life together will build the foundations of their marriage most strongly if they have both learned, through innumerable experiences of this kind, the joy of meeting another's need. Too frequently, hopes of married happiness are dashed because each is seeking his own fulfillment, and then the partner becomes a thing to be used, not a loved person to be joyously served.

Parents find joy in meeting the needs of helpless infants, and their understanding of the child's changing needs grows and deepens as the child grows. And those of us who have lived active lives, working at tasks that seem to us significant, have many precious memories of the deep joy that comes when something we have done has been of use to someone else.

Probably one of the bitterest feelings that often comes with old age is the feeling of being of no further use, incapable of the joy of being needed. No person, however, is ever so completely isolated as to be untouched by any human need. Sometimes we allow the contracting circles of life to harden into a wall behind which we hide, immersed in our own needs, oblivious to the needs of the people around us. But although in old age our contacts may be few, our responsibility to meet human need still exists. Erich Fromm reminds us that the basic definition of responsibility is the *ability to respond*, and that is an ability we can cherish and cultivate to the end of our lives.

Even though the contracting circles have crowded us into a sickroom, we still have a number of contacts.

First of all comes the family. If we are ill at home, we know from past experience what an added burden this means. That it is a burden willingly and lovingly borne is good reason for upwelling gratitude on our part. Is there nothing our family needs from *us* in this situation?

One thing is sure. Bewailing the fact that we are such a care and of no use to anybody does not help. Nor does complaining about unavoidable discomfort and pain. Far better is an attitude of acceptance. (There's that word again; we can't get away from it.) This is a time for the cultivation of sincere and gracious expressions of appreciation for the countless services rendered. The family needs, and is entitled to, the satisfaction of knowing that we are grateful and contented.

What is true of the family is true of friends. When busy people take time out to visit us, either at home or in the hospital, what do they need from us? Surely not a detailed listing of aches and pains and gruesome details of sickbed routines. Maybe they need a friendly ear to listen to *their* troubles. Maybe they need, even more than we do, a few minutes of genuine love and concern focused on them.

Then there is the nurse. With what patient energy she steadily pursues her work of service! What does she need from us? At least courtesy and the refraining from unnecessary demands. Maybe, also, recognition of her as a person, focusing on her rather than on ourselves, or a well earned compliment.

And here comes the doctor. How long is it since he had an uninterrupted night's sleep? What a burden he carries constantly on his heart: the pain his skill is powerless to relieve, the tragedies and heartaches he cannot avert. Is there anything he needs from us? Certainly appreciation is never amiss. Perhaps this morning he also needs an affectionate recognition of his weariness, and maybe even an extra bit of courage on our part to bear necessary pain uncomplainingly, and so make his task easier.

Many of us in our illness look forward to visits from a beloved minister. We know we need him, and the strength and comfort we catch from his contagious faith. But perhaps more than we realize, he needs something from us: a demonstration of the power of religion to strengthen and make joyous even the bitter experiences of life.

Surely it is true, that no matter how contracted the circles may be, no matter how few personal contacts we may have, while life lasts, no one of us is relieved from our responsibility to minister to the needs of others. One other important thing needs to be said: this particular ministry can be performed by no one else. It is an individual assignment, nontransferable.

22

The Earth Is the Lord's!

The earth is the Lord's, and the fulness thereof;
the world, and they that dwell therein. For he
hath founded it upon the seas, and established it
upon the floods. (Psalm 24:1-2)

How we need to hold fast to that affirmation today! The
Christian faith approaches life with a brave recognition of
evil, but never, perhaps, has it taken more conviction than it
does today to affirm unconditionally "The earth is the
Lord's."

What about the incredible instruments for destruction in
the hands of sometimes irresponsible governments? What
about whole populations starving in a world of potential
plenty? What about disease-ravaged communities where
men, women, and little children are suffering and dying
needlessly of diseases which present medical knowledge

could eliminate? What about a generation of young people cut adrift from age-old mores and taboos, desperately searching for new values, new anchorages? What about the thousands of black people in our own and other countries caught in a desperate struggle for a life of dignity and self-respect?

We look in vain for any clear answer to these and similar questions. But faith still declares, "There *is* an answer! The earth is the Lord's!"

We may achieve some glimmerings of insight when we sense, however dimly, that a world without evil would also be a world totally lacking in spiritual values. Without contact with suffering, there could be no compassion; without struggle, no triumph; without need, no response in sacrificial service; without treachery, and deceit, and hatred, no loyalty and trustworthiness and love.

This much we may partly understand, recognizing that our knowledge and comprehension are still microscopic compared with the vastness of God's wisdom and the hidden scope of His eternal purposes. Beyond this, we simply affirm, "The earth is the Lord's . . . and they that dwell therein."

23

I Have Sinned

Few people live to enter the last quarter century of life without having a keen awareness of sin. How seldom we hear the word nowadays! And how we resist it when we do! But one of the bitternesses of old age is the sudden realization that life, with its many rich opportunities for significant living, has narrowed down to a mere handful of swiftly passing years. Along with wasted opportunities, many people look back with bitter regret at specific acts of deliberate or unintentional unkindness.

Trying to push these memories out of the consciousness seldom works. It is better, perhaps, to face them, to look at them in all their ugliness, and to confess with the prodigal son, "Father, I have sinned against heaven, and in thy sight, and am no more worthy to be called thy son" (Luke 15:21).

Having made such a confession, the healthy attitude is to accept God's promised forgiveness, and to face forward with renewed determination to do better.

It is helpful at this point to remember Peter and Judas. Both sinned shamefully against their beloved Master. Judas never grasped the comfort of confession and forgiveness and he killed himself. Peter, however, "wept bitterly," then took up his life with renewed determination and lived it to a triumphant conclusion.

24

I Will Fear No Evil

Yea, though I walk through the valley of the
shadow of death, I will fear no evil: for thou art
with me. (Psalm 23:4)

I will *fear* no evil—not old age, not suffering, not illness,
not loneliness, not bereavement, not death! I will *fear* no
evil. Why? *Not* because God's goodness and protective care
will keep evil from happening to me. Evil happens to
everyone; it is an inescapable part of life. I will fear no evil
because "Thou art with me." God's continuing presence and
companionship make it possible to meet the worst that life
can bring with acceptance and triumphant courage.

25

I Will Rejoice

Lack of fear is good; rejoicing is better. Happiness is not an accidental occurrence due to outward circumstances; it is a by-product, the inevitable result of a right relationship to God and to His people.

This is the day which the Lord hath made; we will rejoice and be glad in it. (Psalm 118:24)

I am come that they might have life, and that they might have it more abundantly. (John 10:10)

In every thing give thanks: for this is the will of God in Christ Jesus concerning you. (1 Thessalonians 5:18)

Thankful—for everything?

How easy it is in times of peace and joy, to lift the heart in gratitude to the Source of all our blessings! But this is only the first step in learning to live life in a constant, unwavering spirit of thankfulness. . . . How sadly we recognize in ourselves the tendency to be grateful only for those things which bring us momentary satisfaction, and how slowly we learn to "give thanks always for all things!" Should we not in fact, be thankful for those tragic experiences which, accepted as from God's hand, develop in us those Christlike qualities for the growth of which all life seems to be designed? For those which force on us the recognition of our complete dependence on God's love and awaken in us the realization of His complete sufficiency to meet every need?[1]

---

[1]*From Everlasting to Everlasting: Promises and Prayers Selected from the Bible* Florence M. Taylor (New York: The Seabury Press, 1973) pages 140-141.

26

I Believe in Eternal Life

No consideration of old age can be realistic without dealing with the imminence of death. That is one reality with which every old person, sooner or later, must come to grips.

Of course, long before we have reached the three-quarters of a century mark, we have had innumerable experiences with the death of others. But our own death is something else again.

The fear of death itself is hard to understand. All our experience points to the fact that the actual passing from life to death is usually nothing to dread.

How precious to most of us is a peaceful night's sleep! How fortunate we are to be able to say, "Ah, I slept so well last night!" It is one of our chief desires and delights. So, if death really were what it seems to be—the end of all consciousness, a deep and eternal sleep free from all pain and anxiety—who, having lived to a ripe old age and knowing that inevitably only greater weariness, feebleness and suffering lie ahead, could fail to welcome death as a friend? Who could dread the painless peace of eternal nothingness?

But Christians, believing in the Bible as God's Word to us, have grounds for a far different and more joyful affirmation. We believe Jesus' promise:

> Let not your heart be troubled: ye believe in God, believe also in me. In my Father's house are many mansions: if it were not so, I would have told you. I go to prepare a place for you. And if I go and prepare a place for you, I will come again, and receive you unto myself; that where I am, there ye may be also. (John 14:1-3)

In the face of the actual experiences of life, the death of those dear to us, the apparent end of all consciousness, the destruction of the physical body, in the face of all this, how is it possible to hold fast to a belief in the survival after death of the individual personality? Is it not mere "wishful thinking"?

Science itself, however, has given us a different conception of "destruction." There is, it appears, no such thing. We put water in a pot and set it on the stove. After a while the water disappears. Have we destroyed the water? Not at all. We have merely changed it into vapor.

The green leaves of summer turn brown and shrivel up. They fall from the tree to the ground. They are drenched by the rain and snow, trodden underfoot, and crushed to powder. But are they destroyed? We know they are not; they are merely changed. Their usefulness is far from over. The rich dust will provide food for other leaves on other trees, *ad infinitum.*

We tear up a piece of paper. Have we destroyed it? Not really. We have changed it into a handful of scraps. We burn the scraps, but we have only reduced them to ashes.

Even so evanescent a thing as a candle flame apparently escapes destruction.

> Sir Arthur Keith is one of the great British scientists. Professor Arthur Compton is one of the great American scientists. The first is an utter disbeliever; the second a thorough believer. According to Sir Arthur Keith, when a man dies he goes out like a candle; to which Professor Compton replies that the candle does not go out; its energy goes on and on to the farthest reaches of the universe. Be sure of this: If God is, one way or another our candle does not go out. Its mode of going on may be utterly different from anything we have pictured it to be. Indeed, I am sure that must be so, but one way or another, as Emerson said:
>
> ". . . What is excellent,
>
> As God lives, is permanent."
>
> And in manners and fashions beyond our power to imagine the candle does not go out.[1]

---

[1]Harry Emerson Fosdick, "Life's Candle Does Not Go Out," in *Treasury of the Christian Faith*, Stanley I. Stuber and Thomas C. Clark, eds. (New York: Association Press, 1949) p. 425.

If then, destruction, even of physical matter, really is *not* destruction at all, but merely transformation, what shall we think of the endurance of reality that is not physical? *Is* there any such reality? Or shall we believe that *all* there is to this beloved minister who has spread the contagion of his joyous faith to hundreds of people is his body? Absurd! Or this mother, whose years have been a continuous self-sacrifice to provide for her family—is her body all there is to her?

Christians hold to the belief that in some mysterious and inexplicable way, personality is *more* than the mere physical body which clothes it, and so we entertain frankly and without embarrassment the hope that this human personality, this spiritual reality, may prove to be as indestructible as matter.

We believe in the resurrection of Jesus from the dead, and in the Bible teachings about eternal life:

> Jesus said: Verily, verily, I say unto you, He that heareth my word, and believeth on him that sent me, hath everlasting life, and shall not come into condemnation: but is passed from death to life. (John 5:24)
> Eternal life is not something into which we shall enter when we die: it is, on the contrary, a quality of living available to us in the present world.[2]
> And this is life eternal, that they might know thee the only true God, and Jesus Christ, whom thou hast sent. (John 17:3)
> He who lives in constant awareness of God,

---

[2]*In the Morning, Bread: Devotions for the New Day*, selected by Florence M. Taylor (New Canaan, Conn., Keats Publishing, Inc. 1976.) Day 228.

whose "meat is to do the will" of his heavenly Father, who has totally surrendered himself and all his abilities, his thoughts and words and deeds to God's guidance, is living the life eternal *now*. And to the extent in which we approach that goal, we have already entered into the fulfillment of the promise of eternal life.[3]

If that which ye have heard from the beginning shall remain in you, ye also shall continue in the Son, and in the Father. And this is the promise that he hath promised us, even eternal life. (1 John 2:24-25)

I believe in eternal life. I shall die fully expecting some indefinable, indescribable continuation of life, in which I shall still be recognizably myself, although I would hope for infinite possibilities of improvement!

Two wise old men have contributed to this faith of mine. The first is John Quincy Adams.

One day when John Quincy Adams was eighty years of age a friend met him on the streets of Boston. "How is John Quincy Adams?" this friend asked gaily. The old man's eye began to twinkle, and then he spoke slowly. His words have become classic. "John Quincy Adams himself is very well, thank you. But the house he lives in is sadly dilapidated. It is tottering on its foundations. The walls are badly shattered, and the roof is worn.

[3]*Ibid.* Day 228.

The building trembles with every wind, and I think John Quincy Adams will have to move out of it before long. But he himself is very well." And with a wave of the hand the old man walked on.[4]

The second is Benjamin Franklin. Here is his epitaph, as he wrote it:

> The Body of Benjamin Franklin,
> Printer,
> Like the Covering of an old Book,
> Its Contents torn out,
> And stript of its Lettering and Gilding,
> Lies here, Food for Worms;
> But the Work shall not be lost,
> It will (as he believed) appear once more,
> In a new and more beautiful Edition,
> Corrected and amended
> By the Author.[5]

---

[4]J.G. Gilkey, "Old Age and Immortality," in *Treasury of the Christian Faith*, Stanley I. Stuber and Thomas C. Clark, eds. (New York: Association Press, 1949) p. 421.

[5]*Stories on Stone: A Book of American Epitaphs*, Charles L. Wallis, ed. (New York: Oxford University Press, 1954), p. 137.